Disney FROZEN

MUSIC Activity Book

An Introduction to Music

Compiled and Edited by Sharon Stosur

Disney Characters and Artwork © 2020 Disney

ISBN 978-1-5400-8373-9

Visit Hal Leonard Online at
www.halleonard.com

Contact us:
Hal Leonard
7777 West Bluemound Road
Milwaukee, WI 53213
Email: info@halleonard.com

In Europe, contact:
Hal Leonard Europe Limited
42 Wigmore Street
Marylebone, London, W1U 2RN
Email: info@halleonardeurope.com

In Australia, contact:
Hal Leonard Australia Pty. Ltd.
4 Lentara Court
Cheltenham, Victoria, 3192 Australia
Email: info@halleonard.com.au

Hi! I'm Olaf, and this is the **DISNEY FROZEN MUSIC ACTIVITY BOOK**. If you're new to reading music and playing the piano, that's okay! We'll start at the beginning. Elsa, Anna, Kristoff and I will be here to help. We'll learn about music and play and sing some of your favorite songs from *Frozen* and *Frozen 2*. In addition to the songs there are plenty of games, puzzles, and other activities to enjoy. Let's get started!

An Introduction to Music

Contents

The Staff

When people sing or play music on an instrument, the sound they make can be written down with musical symbols called **notes**. Notes can be put together, one by one, to make a song.

To make it easier to see which notes are higher or lower than others, music notes are written on a set of five lines and four spaces called a **staff**. At the beginning of the staff is a **clef sign** to name the lines and spaces. The clef sign we use in this book is called **Treble Clef**.

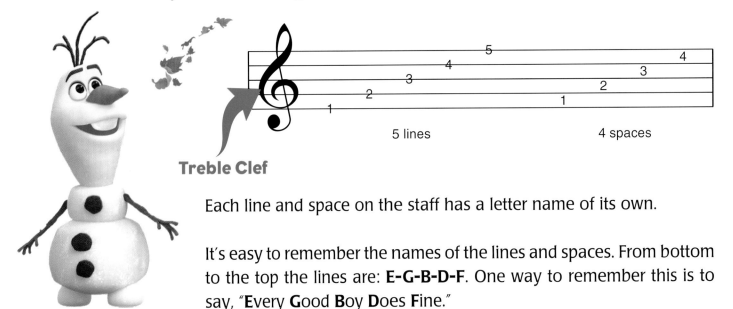

Treble Clef

Each line and space on the staff has a letter name of its own.

It's easy to remember the names of the lines and spaces. From bottom to the top the lines are: **E-G-B-D-F**. One way to remember this is to say, "**E**very **G**ood **B**oy **D**oes **F**ine."

From bottom to top the spaces are: **F-A-C-E**. This is easy to remember because the names of the spaces spell "face."

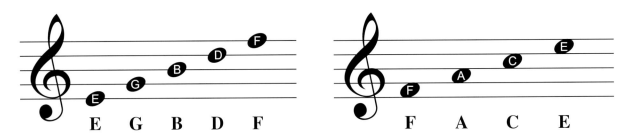

If a note is too high or too low to fit on the staff, extra lines can be added. These short lines are called **ledger lines**.

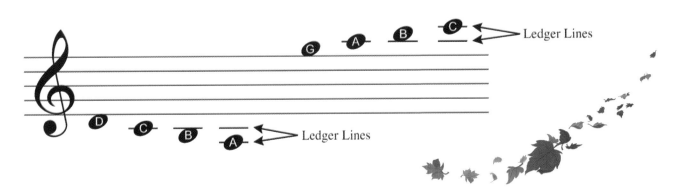

Notes on the Staff

These notes on the staff spell words. Place the notes on the correct line or space.
The first one is done for you.

F   A   D   E   D   A   C   E

F   E   D   E   G   G   D   A   D

B   A   G   G   A   G   E   B   E   A   D

D   E   E   D   F   A   C   E   D

B   A   D   G   E   C   A   G   E

Answers on page 72

The Keyboard

It's easy to play notes on the piano keyboard. The keyboard is organized in groups of black keys and white keys. Take a look at the keyboard below to see the pattern of black key groups.

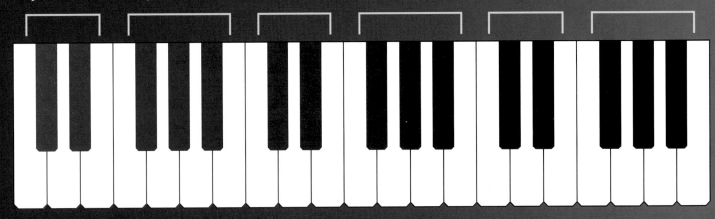

The white keys are named just like the notes on the staff, using the seven letters of the music alphabet.

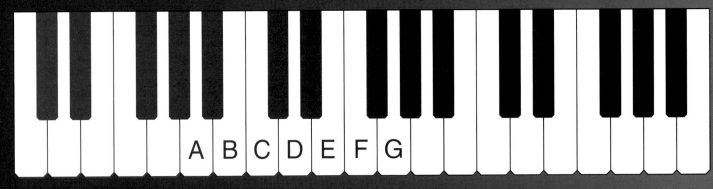

Name the Keys

Practice naming the white keys on the keyboards below.
Label all the Cs, Ds, and Es. These notes touch the groups of two black keys.

Label all the Fs, Gs, As, and Bs. These notes touch the groups of three black keys.

Fill in the names of the missing keys:

C _ E F _ _ B _ D _ _ G A _ C D _ _ _ _ B

Finger Numbers

Finger numbers tell us which finger to use when we play notes on the keyboard. We number the fingers 1–5, and thumb is always number 1.

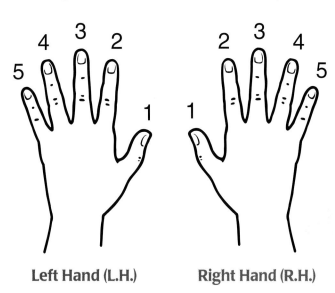

Left Hand (L.H.)   **Right Hand (R.H.)**

Play the first phrase of the chorus of "Let It Go" using finger numbers. Start with your right-hand thumb on G, as illustrated on the small keyboard below. Remember, G is found near the group of three black keys.

G	A	B	C	D
1	2	3	4	5

Let It Go

A	B	C	G	G	D	C
2	3	4	1	1	5	4
Let	it	go,	let	it	go,	can't

A	A	A	A	B	C
2	2	2	2	3	4
hold	it	back	an	y	more.

Reading and Playing Music on the Staff

Here's the first phrase to Kristoff's song, "Reindeer(s) Are Better Than People."

Remember the names of the lines and spaces or refer back to page 4 for a review. Be patient with yourself as you learn the names of the notes. And remember, the note names appear inside each note! There are small finger numbers above the notes. They tell you which fingers to use to play each note.

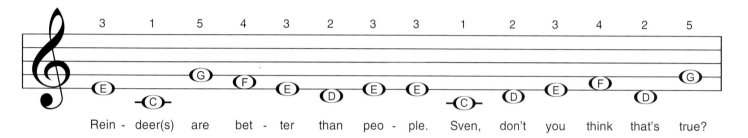

Rein - deer(s) are bet - ter than peo - ple. Sven, don't you think that's true?

Note Values

A music note on a staff shows two things: how high or low a sound is, and how long the sound lasts.

Each type of note has a specific rhythmic value. Note values are measured in **beats**. When you tap your foot or clap your hands along with a song, you are tapping or clapping the beat.

When the quarter note gets one beat, all other rhythmic values are determined by the quarter note.

Quarter Note
A quarter note lasts for one beat.

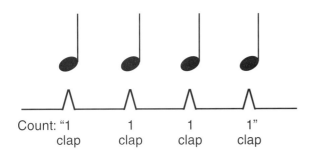

Count: "1   1   1   1"
      clap   clap   clap   clap

Half Note
A half note fills the time of two quarter notes.

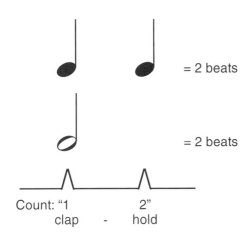

= 2 beats

= 2 beats

Count: "1   2"
      clap   -   hold

Dotted Half Note

A dotted half notes fills the time of three quarter notes.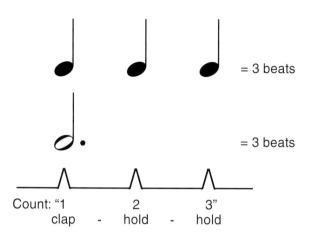

= 3 beats

= 3 beats

Count: "1   2   3"
clap - hold - hold

Whole Note

A whole note fills the time of four quarter notes.

= 4 beats

= 4 beats

Count: "1   2   3   4"
clap - hold - hold - hold

Here's the first phrase of "Reindeer(s) Are Better Than People" written in rhythm.

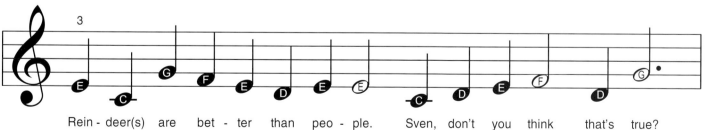

Rein - deer(s) are bet - ter than peo - ple. Sven, don't you think that's true?

Coloring Fun

Use the note values to color Elsa and Anna.

If the note equals **4 beats**, color those areas **yellow**.

If the note equals **3 beats**, color those areas **orange**.

If the note equals **2 beats**, color those areas **blue**.

If the note equals **1 beat**, color those areas **pink/magenta**

How Music Is Organized

You already know about the staff, which shows you how high or low the notes are. Here's the staff with some added music symbols to help you read the notes. You'll always find a **clef** sign at the beginning of each line of music. **Bar lines** divide the staff into **measures**, which contain groups of beats. Right next to the clef sign is a **time signature**. The top number tells you how many beats are in each measure. The number four on the bottom reminds you that a quarter note equals one beat. There is a **double bar line** at the end of the final measure. This sign tells you where the song ends.

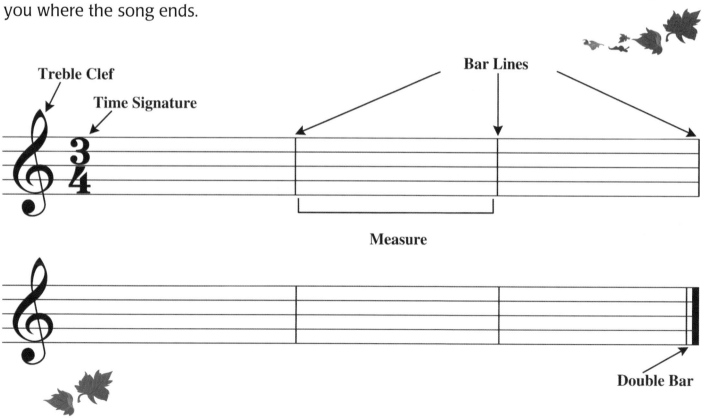

Counting Notes in $\frac{4}{4}$ Time

"Vuelie" from FROZEN has a $\frac{4}{4}$ **time signature**. The number 4 on top means there are four beats in each measure. Tap your foot or count along with the numbers "1-2-3-4" for each measure to make sure that you keep a steady beat.

"Vuelie" is a traditional Sami *yoik*. A *yoik* is both a type of song and the unique vocal style used to perform it, similar to chanting. A translation of the title would be "Song of the Earth."

Vuelie

Written by Frode Fjellheim
and Christophe Beck

4 beats per measure

Moderately slow

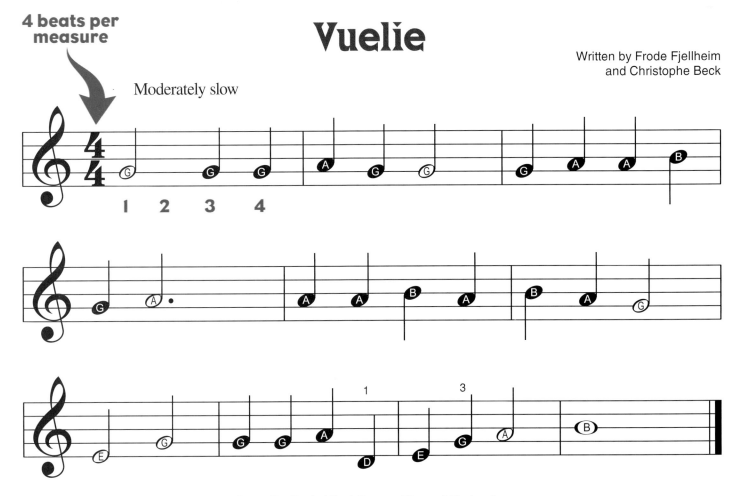

Add the Missing Bar Lines

Bar lines divide music into **measures**. The **time signature** tells us how many beats are in each measure.

First, note the time signature in each example. How many beats should be in each measure? Divide each example in measures using bar lines.

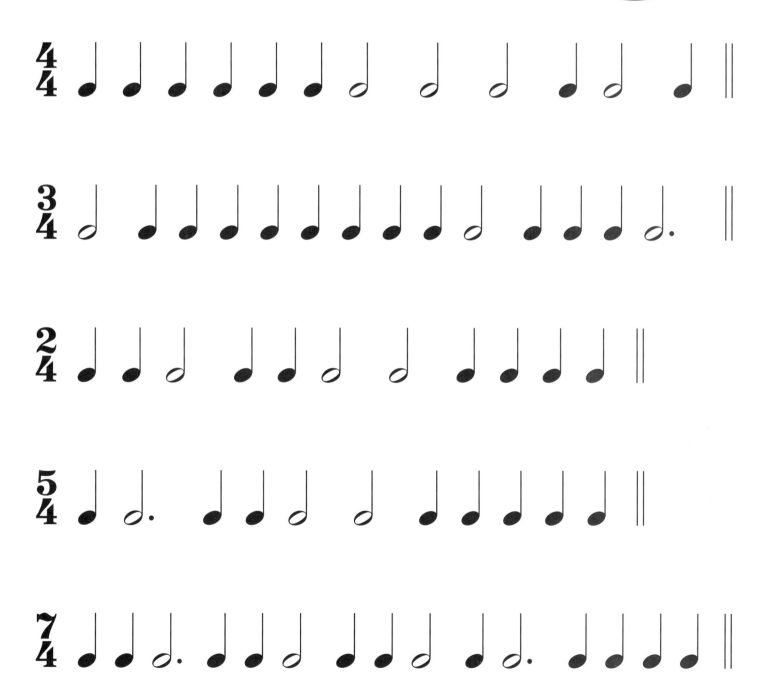

Answers on page 72

Rests

Rests are music symbols that stand for silence. A rest will indicate when *not* to play a note. Like notes, each rest is worth a certain number of beats, as shown below.

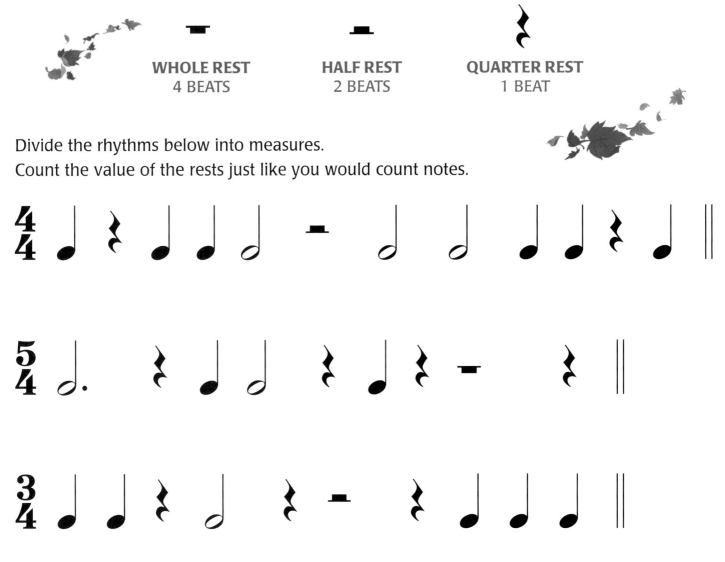

WHOLE REST
4 BEATS

HALF REST
2 BEATS

QUARTER REST
1 BEAT

Divide the rhythms below into measures.
Count the value of the rests just like you would count notes.

Ties

Earlier in the book you learned that a whole note is our longest note, and that it lasts four beats. Then how do composers write longer notes? They use **ties**. Ties are curved lines that connect two or more of the same note name to make longer notes. The tied notes must be on the same line or in the same space. The first note is played or sung and held for the full value of all the tied notes. Play and count the example below.

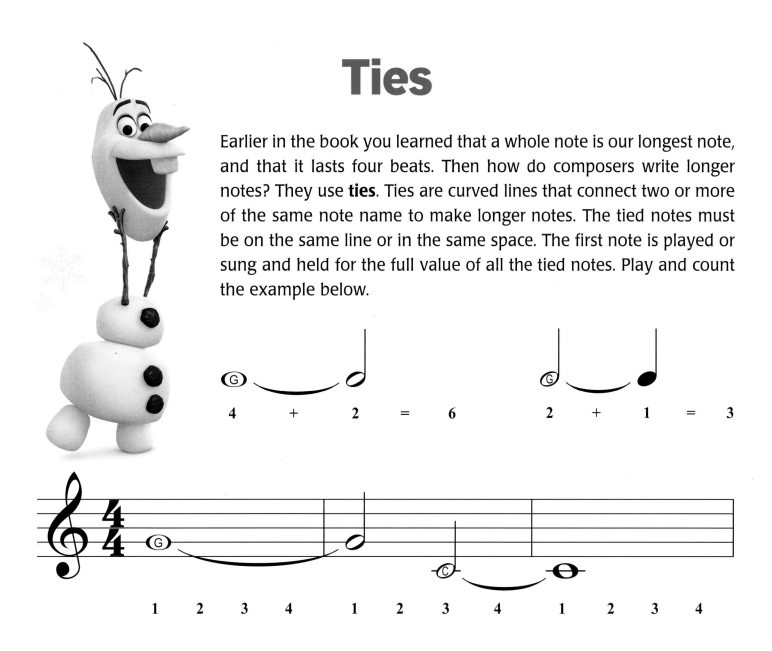

Dynamics

Dynamics are symbols for how softly or loudly music is played. Often the words are in Italian. Here are some common dynamics, and what they mean.

There are other symbols in music that help you play expressively. One of those symbols is **rit.**, which is short for **ritardando**, meaning to slow the music slightly. You'll often see this at the end of a song. Slow the music slightly to bring the song to a gentle ending. **Tempo markings** tell us about the speed and character of a song. These are found at the beginning of the song, right above the time signature.

Eighth Notes

So far, you've learned about quarter notes, half notes, dotted half notes, and whole notes. Here's something new: eighth notes!

One eighth note looks like a quarter note with a flag. When two or more eighth notes appear together, the flags turn into beams. When the time signature is $\frac{4}{4}$, eighth notes are often connected in groups of two or four. The beams make reading the eighth notes easier. Two eighth notes fill the time of one quarter note, or one beat.

If a quarter note is one beat long, how long is an eighth note?

An eighth note is half a beat long.

Uh...what's a half beat?

When you count eighth notes and half beats, it's easier if you think about tapping your foot to the music. Look at Kristoff's boot, tapping along with the quarter notes. We count the quarter notes 1-2-3-4.

As Kristoff taps, his foot moves up and down, tapping on the floor for each quarter note beat. To count eighth notes, he taps the same way but the notes sound twice as fast. Two eighth notes equal one quarter note.

Count: 1 & 2 & 3 & 4 &

The "ands" are when he raises his foot.

Try it yourself, tapping your foot and counting **1 & 2 & 3 & 4 &**

Clap and count the rhythm below from the song, "Do You Want to Build a Snowman?" There is an eighth rest in measure 3. An eighth rest ♪ has the same value as an eighth note.

Let It Go

Music and Lyrics by Kristen Anderson-Lopez
and Robert Lopez

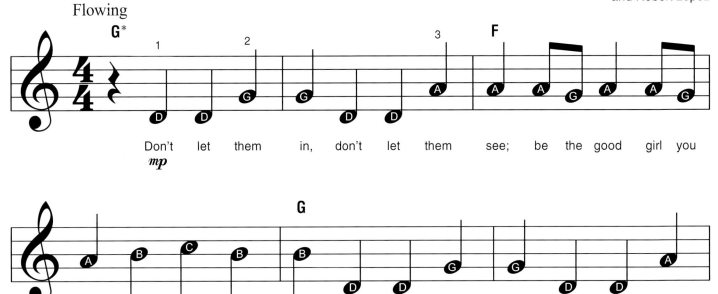

Don't let them in, don't let them see; be the good girl you

al - ways have to be. Con - ceal, don't feel, don't let them

know... _____ Well, now they know. _____

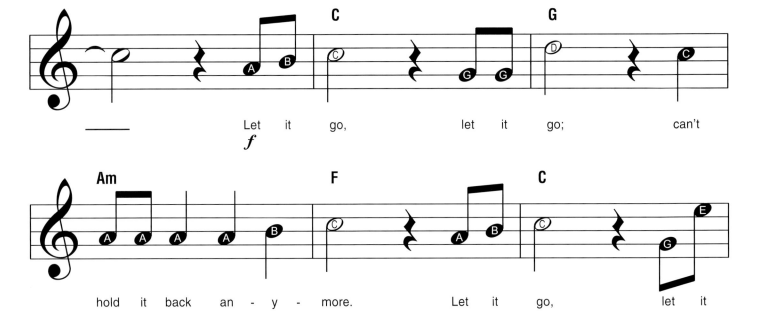

Let it go, let it go; can't

hold it back an - y - more. Let it go, let it

*Above the staff are letters representing chords. These can be used
by someone to play along with you on the guitar or keyboard.

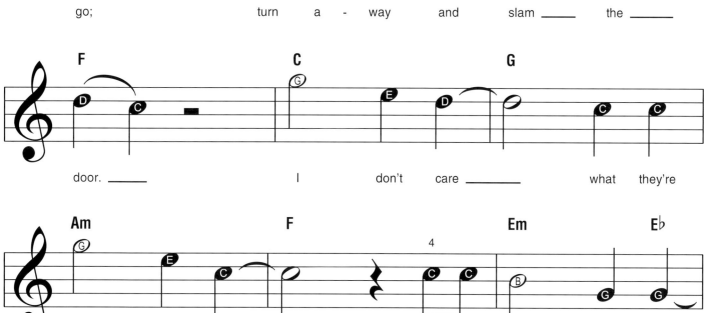

G				Am				

go;   turn a - way and   slam ____ the ____

F			C			G		

door. ____   I   don't care _____   what they're

Am			F			Em		Eb

going   to   say; _____   let the storm rage on. ____

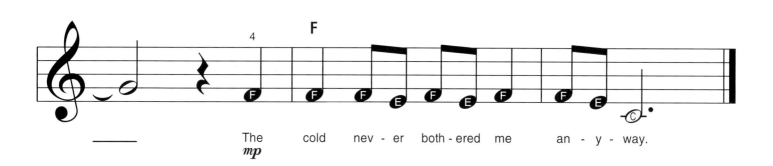

____   The   cold nev - er both - ered me   an - y - way.
mp

21

Dotted Notes

Another way to make a note last longer is to add a dot. Adding a dot to a note adds half the value of the note it follows. It's kind of like playing a tied note without the tie.

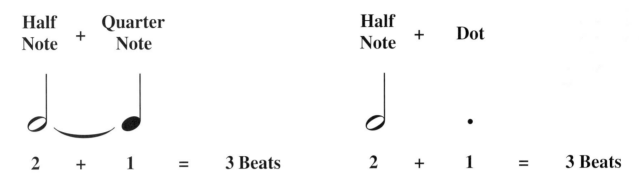

You can add a dot to any note to increase its value. When you add a dot to a quarter note, you add half a beat.

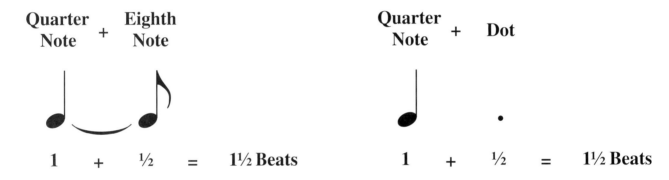

A dotted quarter note is often followed by an eighth note. Here are some dotted note rhythms to practice. Clap and count. You may wish to tap your foot to keep the beat.

Sharps

As you know, there are both white and black keys on the piano keyboard. So far, we've been playing songs using only the white keys. Let's learn how to name the black keys and find them on the keyboard.

Here's a new music symbol, the **sharp sign**: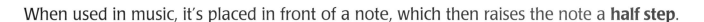

When used in music, it's placed in front of a note, which then raises the note a **half step**.

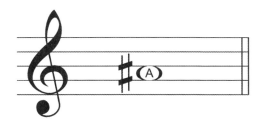

A half step is a very small distance in music. On the keyboard, we describe it as one key to the very next key. Sharped notes are usually between two musical letter names. For example, A♯ is between A and B. This is easiest to see on the keyboard, where sharp notes are usually black keys.

> Remember, when you see a sharp in front of a note, play or sing a half step higher. A note with a sharp sounds a little higher than the same note without a sharp.

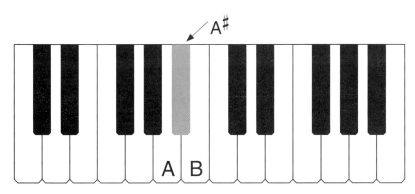

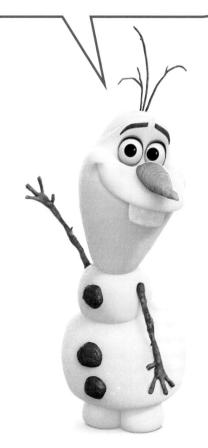

Do You Want to Build a Snowman?

Here we begin with *pick-up* notes, played before the first full measure of music.

Music and Lyrics by Kristen Anderson-Lopez
and Robert Lopez

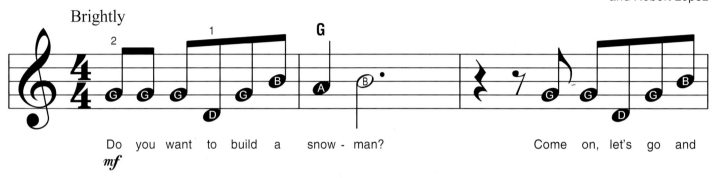

Do you want to build a snow-man? Come on, let's go and

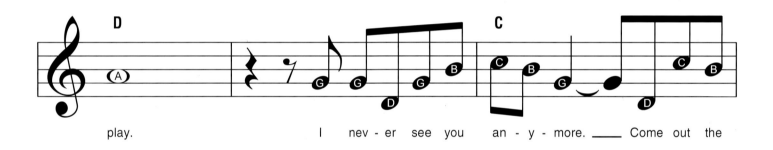

play. I nev-er see you an-y-more. ____ Come out the

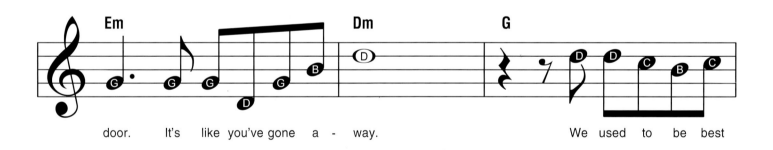

door. It's like you've gone a-way. We used to be best

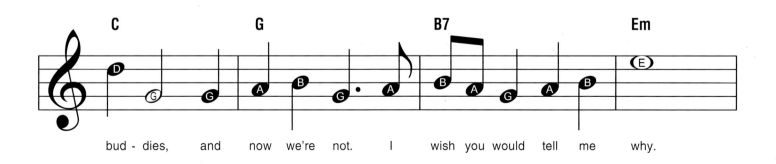

bud-dies, and now we're not. I wish you would tell me why.

Do you want to build a snow - man?

It does - n't have to be a

snow - man.

(Go away, Anna.) O - kay, bye.

Note Reading Review

Name the notes and color Olaf, Anna, Elsa, Sven, and Kristoff with crayons, pencils, or markers using the note and color key at the bottom of the page.

orange   **purple**   **brown**   **yellow**   **red**   **light blue**

Reindeer(s) Are Better Than People

Music and Lyrics by
Kristen Anderson-Lopez and Robert Lopez

Freely

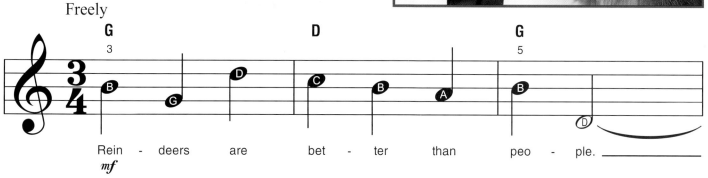

Rein - deers are bet - ter than peo - ple. _____

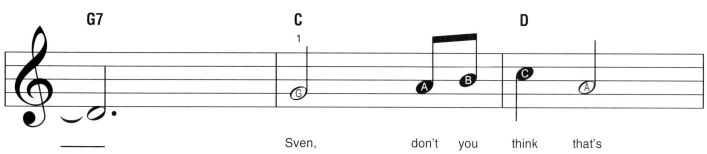

_____ Sven, don't you think that's

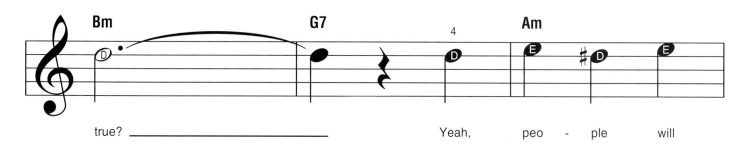

true? _____ Yeah, peo - ple will

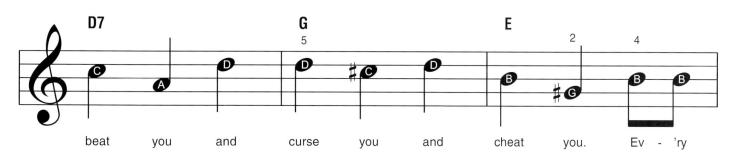

beat you and curse you and cheat you. Ev - 'ry

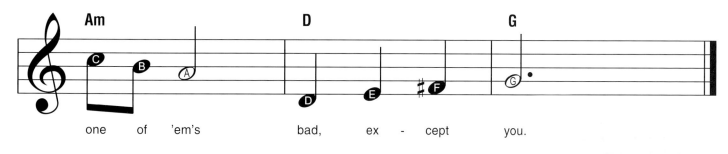

one of 'em's bad, ex - cept you.

Flats

In the next song, "Some Things Never Change," you'll see a note with a flat in front of it, like this:

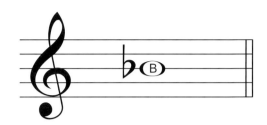

A note with a flat in front of it is a half step *lower* than it would be without the flat.

The flat is added to the name of the note. In this example, the name of the note is not B anymore, it's **B-flat**, also written **B♭**.

Just like sharps, flat notes usually fall between two letter name notes. For example, **B♭** is between A and B. On keyboard instruments, flat notes are usually black keys.

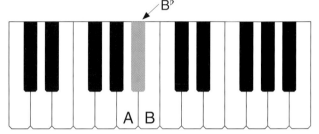

Wait a minute! Before you said that A♯ is between A and B. Now you're saying that B♭ is between A and B! Are you trying to get me mixed up?

No, we're not trying to get Elsa mixed up. That black key between A and B can be called either sharp or flat. Check out the keyboard below. The black keys get their name from the white keys. When going *up* the keyboard, the black keys have "sharp" names. When going *down* the keyboard, the black keys have "flat" names.

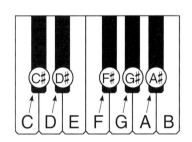

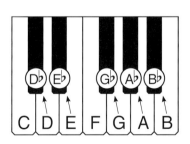

Just remember: when you see a **flat** in front of a note, play the very next note **lower** on the keyboard. When you see a **sharp** in front of a note, play the very next note **higher** on the keyboard.

Some Things Never Change

Music and Lyrics by
Kristen Anderson-Lopez and Robert Lopez

Sharp or Flat?

Placing a sharp in front of a note **raises** the pitch a half step. Add sharps to these notes. Be sure to place the sharp sign in front of the note. The "center square" of the sharp sign includes the line or space of the note.

Placing a flat in front of a note **lowers** the pitch a half step. Add flat signs to these notes. Place the round part of the flat sign carefully to include the line or space of the note.

Name the following sharp and flat notes.

1. ____   2. ____   3. ____   4. ____   5. ____

6. ____   7. ____   8. ____   9. ____   10. ____

Answers on page 72

Crossword Fun

ACROSS

5. Flats _____ a note a half-step.
6. The _____ half note lasts for three beats.
8. Sharps _____ a note a half-step.
11. A _____ note lasts two beats.
12. Adding a dot to a note _____ its value.
13. The _____ number of a time signature tells you how many beats are in a measure.
15. A _____ is the space between two bar lines.
17. A _____ clef appears at the beginning of a song.
18. _____ are symbols that stand for silence.

DOWN

1. The notes that fall in the four spaces of the treble clef spell _____.
2. A _____ is a curved line that connects two notes with the same pitch.
3. A whole note lasts _____ beats.
4. Notes are written on a _____ which has five lines.
7. A _____ appears at the end of the final measure of a song. *(2 words)*
9. The letters of the music alphabet are: _____.
10. Two _____ notes take the time of one quarter note.
14. Notes that are too high or too low to fit on the staff are written using _____ lines.
16. Eighth notes can be written with flags or _____.

Answers on page 72

Music Math

Let's do some music math! Add the values of the tied notes to find the answer to each of these musical equations. The first one is done for you. Check your answers on page 72.

1.

♩ ⌣ ♩

_2_ + _1_ = _3_

2.

♩ ⌣ ♩ ⌣ ♩ ⌣ ♩

___ + ___ + ___ + ___ = ___

3.

♩ ⌣ 𝅝

___ + ___ = ___

4.

♩ ⌣ ♩ ⌣ ♩ ⌣ ♩

___ + ___ + ___ + ___ = ___

5.

𝅝 ⌣ ♩ ♩ ⌣ ♩

___ + ___ + ___ = ___

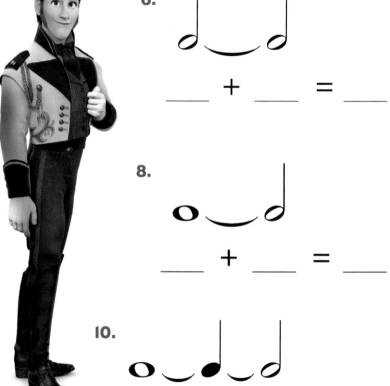

6.

♩ ⌣ ♩

___ + ___ = ___

7.

♩ ⌣ ♩ ⌣ ♩

___ + ___ + ___ = ___

8.

𝅝 ⌣ ♩

___ + ___ = ___

9.

𝅝 ⌣ 𝅝

___ + ___ = ___

10.

𝅝 ⌣ ♩ ⌣ ♩

___ + ___ + ___ = ___

Syncopation

In many rhythm patterns, the strongest beat occurs on the first beat of the measure.

In $\frac{4}{4}$ time, the strong beats fall on one and three.

When beats other than these receive a strong accent, we hear **syncopation**. Syncopation in music is when an accent occurs on what is usually a weak beat in the measure. One of the most common syncopated rhythms is when an eighth note is played on beat one, followed by a quarter note.

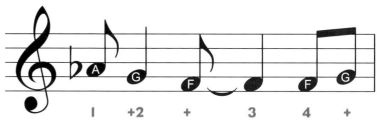

Sometimes syncopation occurs when a note is tied.

Show Yourself

Music and Lyrics by Kristen Anderson-Lopez
and Robert Lopez

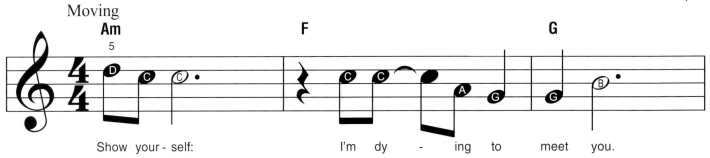

Show your-self: I'm dy - ing to meet you.

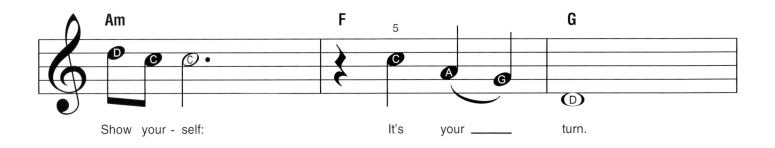

Show your-self: It's your ___ turn.

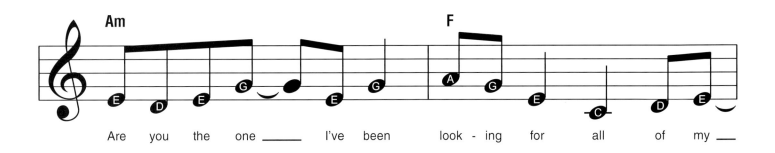

Are you the one ___ I've been look - ing for all of my ___

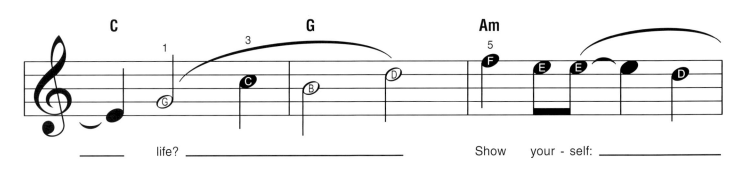

___ life? ___ Show your - self: ___

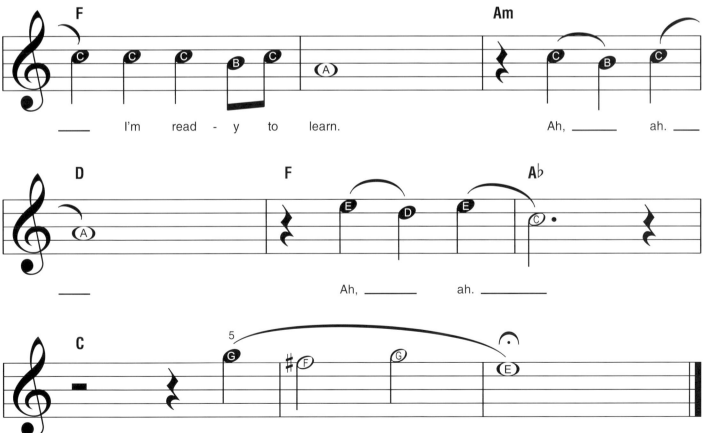

_____ I'm read - y to learn.

Ah, _____ ah. _____

Ah, _____ ah. _____

Ah. _____

Lost in the Woods

Music and Lyrics by
Kristen Anderson-Lopez and Robert Lopez

Moderately

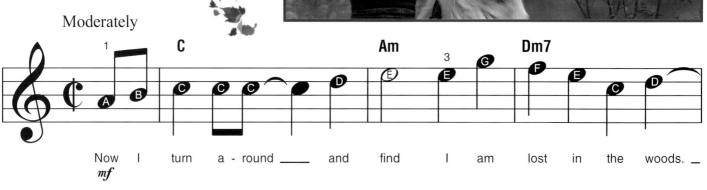

Now I turn a-round ____ and find I am lost in the woods. ____
mf

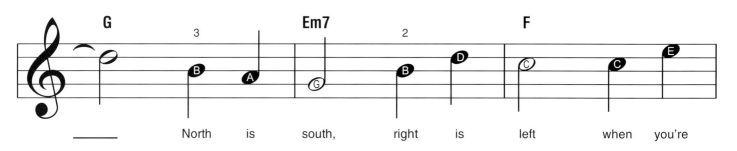

____ North is south, right is left when you're

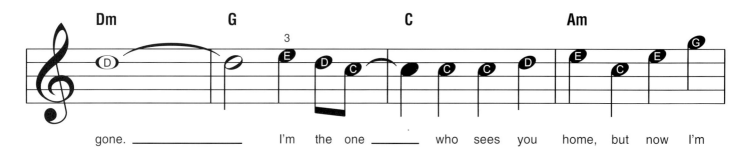

gone. _____ I'm the one ____ who sees you home, but now I'm

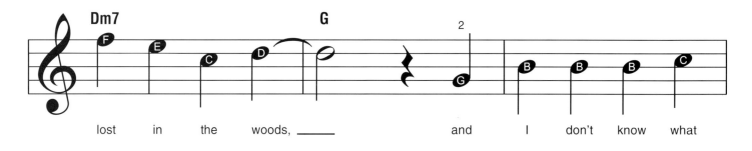

lost in the woods, ____ and I don't know what

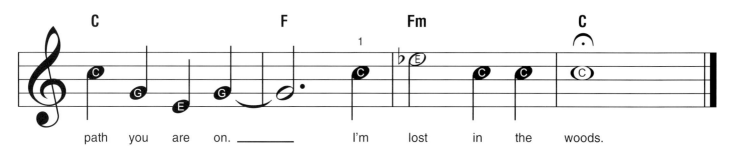

path you are on. _____ I'm lost in the woods.

More Music Signs and Symbols

A **Repeat Sign** tells you to go back and play a portion of the song again. When this happens, often there is more than one set of words (verses) below the melody notes.

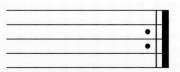

Sometimes a whole section of music can be repeated, ending in a slightly different way the second time. This is indicated by **repeat signs**, and **1st and 2nd ending signs**. Let's look at "All Is Found" on the next page. Play from the beginning to the repeat sign. The measure leading up to the repeat sign is marked with a first ending sign. Now go back to the first repeat sign. Play these measures again, skip the first ending this time and play the second ending measures instead. Continue playing until you reach the words, **D.S. al Coda**. Now return to the **Sign** 𝄋 at the beginning of the song and play until the words **To Coda** ⊕. Jump to the section marked **Coda** and play to the end.

All Is Found

Music and Lyrics by Kristen Anderson-Lopez
and Robert Lopez

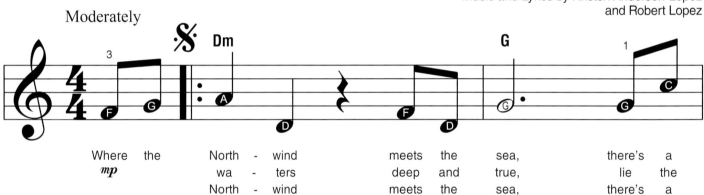

Where the North - wind meets the sea, there's a
mp wa - ters deep and true, lie the
North - wind meets the sea, there's a

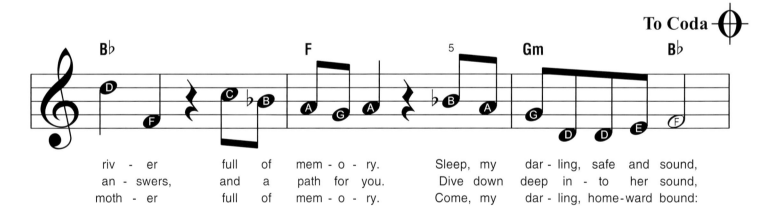

riv - er full of mem - o - ry. Sleep, my dar - ling, safe and sound,
an - swers, and a path for you. Dive down deep in - to her sound,
moth - er full of mem - o - ry. Come, my dar - ling, home-ward bound:

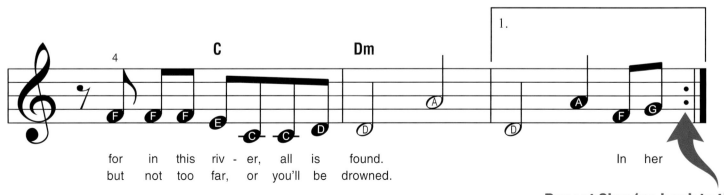

for in this riv - er, all is found.   In her
but not too far, or you'll be drowned.

Repeat Sign (go back to the beginning and play again)

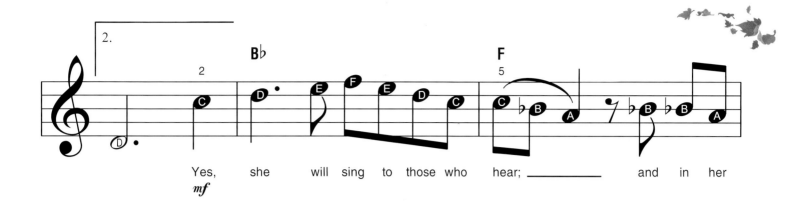

Yes, she will sing to those who hear; ___ and in her

mf

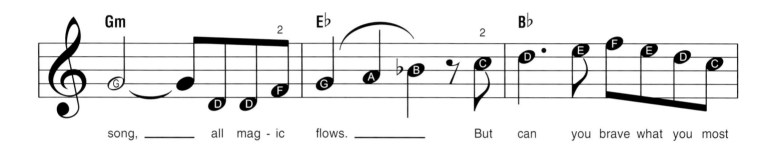

song, ___ all mag - ic flows. ___ But can you brave what you most

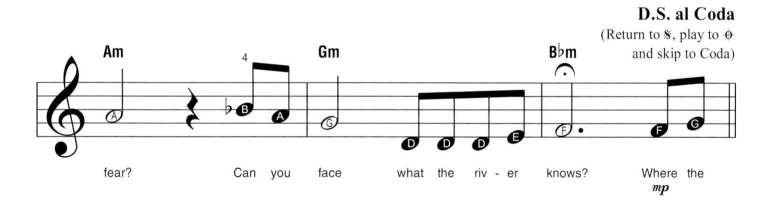

D.S. al Coda
(Return to 𝄋, play to ⊕
and skip to Coda)

fear? Can you face what the riv - er knows? Where the

mp

CODA

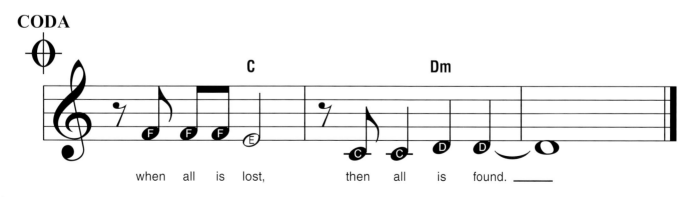

when all is lost, then all is found. ___

Triplets

A **triplet** divides a quarter note into 3 equal parts.

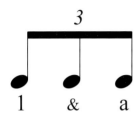

Count triplets "1 & a"

1   &   a

Notice how easily you can see the beats when there are several triplets in a row.

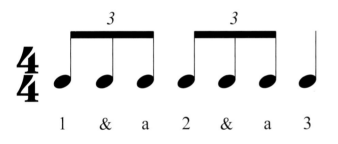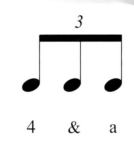

1 & a 2 & a 3 & 4 & a

Practice triplets by clapping and counting the rhythms below.

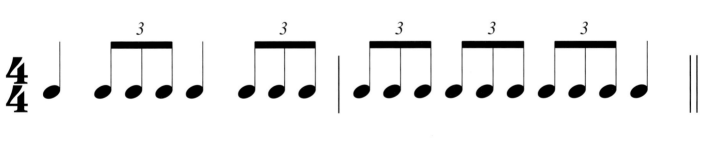

Complete the measures below. Use at least one triplet in each example.

In Summer

Music and Lyrics by Kristen Anderson-Lopez
and Robert Lopez

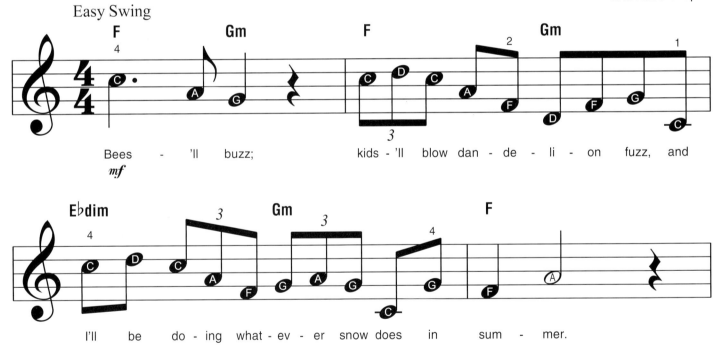

Bees-'ll buzz; kids-'ll blow dan-de-li-on fuzz, and

I'll be do-ing what-ev-er snow does in sum-mer.

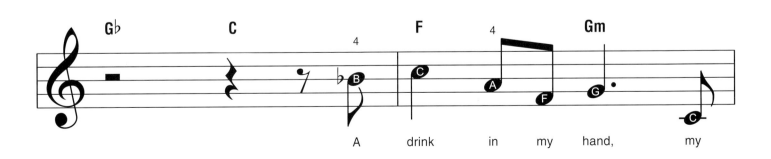

A drink in my hand, my

snow up a-gainst the burn-ing sand, prob-'ly get-ting gor-geous-ly tanned in

sum - mer. _____ I'll fi - n'lly see a sum-mer breeze blow a -

way a win-ter storm, ____ and find out what hap-pens to sol - id wa-ter when

it gets warm. ____ And I

can't wait to see what my bud-dies all think of me. Just im -

ag - ine how much cool - er I'll be in sum - mer! _____

Maze Fun

Help Kristoff and Sven find Anna.

Reindeer(s) Are Better Than People (Cont.)

Music and Lyrics by Kristen Anderson-Lopez
and Robert Lopez

Freely

Rein - deers are bet - ter than peo - ple.

Sven, why is love so hard? *(Spoken:) You*

feel what you feel, and those feel - ings are real.

Come on, Kris - toff, let down your guard.

16th Notes

In music, a quarter note beat can be divided into smaller values.
These notes receive fractions, or parts of the beat.

Four **16th notes** take up the time of one quarter note.

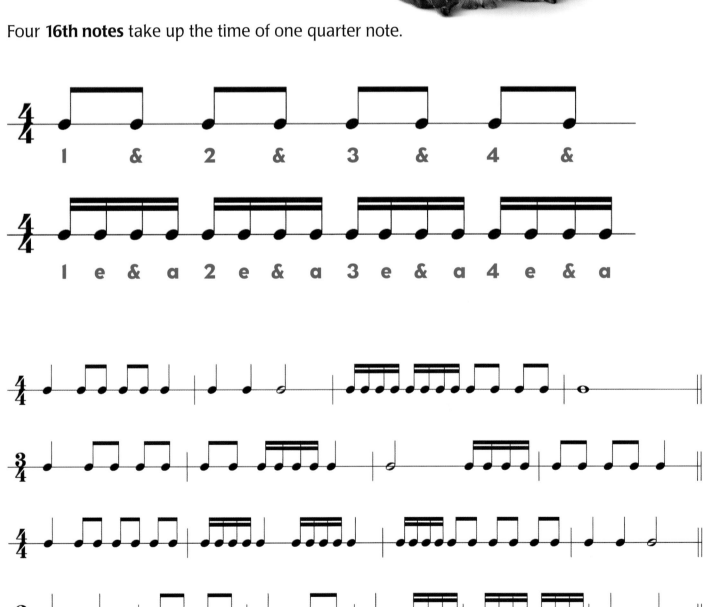

Rest Review

Every note has a corresponding rest.
Review the chart below.

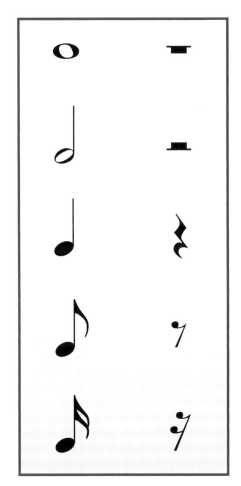

True or False?

Circle T for true or F for false after considering the following music math equations.

1. T F ♪♪ = ♩

2. T F 𝄀𝄐 = ♩

3. T F ♪♪ + ♩ = ♩

4. T F 𝄀𝄐 + ♪♪ = ♩

5. T F 𝄾 + ♪ + ♩ = 𝅝

6. T F 𝄀𝄐 = ♪♪

7. T F 𝄾 + 𝄾 = ♩

8. T F 𝄿 + 𝄿 + 𝄾 = ♩

9. T F 𝄀𝄐 + ♩ = 𝅝

10. T F ♪ + ♪ + 𝄾 = 𝅝

Answers on page 72.

Love Is an Open Door

Music and Lyrics by Kristen Anderson-Lopez
and Robert Lopez

Fixer Upper

Music and Lyrics by Kristen Anderson-Lopez
and Robert Lopez

With comic bounce

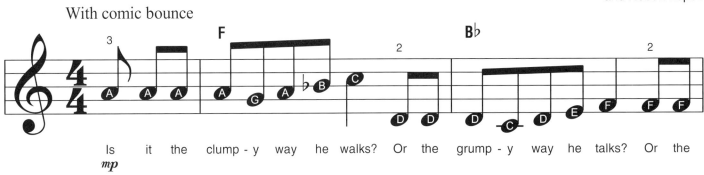

Is it the clump - y way he walks? Or the grump - y way he talks? Or the

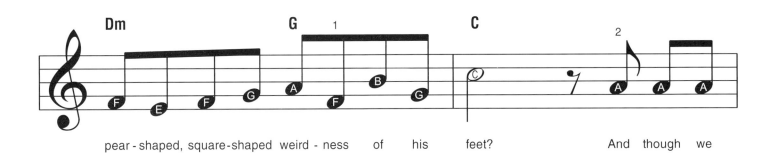

pear - shaped, square-shaped weird - ness of his feet? And though we

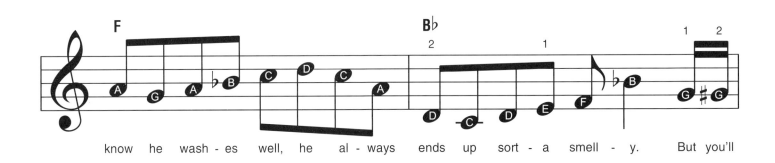

know he wash - es well, he al - ways ends up sort - a smell - y. But you'll

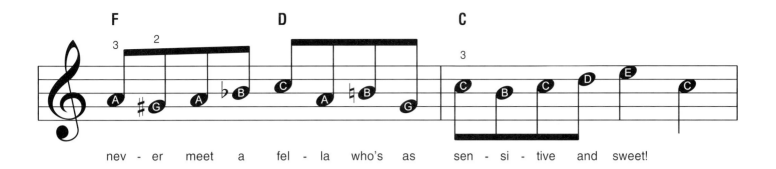

nev - er meet a fel - la who's as sen - si - tive and sweet!

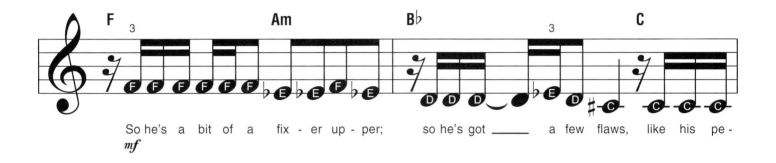

So he's a bit of a fix - er up - per; so he's got _____ a few flaws, like his pe -

mf

cu - liar brain, dear, his thing with the rein - deer, that's a lit - tle out - side of na - ture's laws!

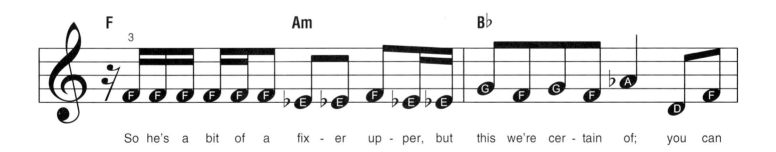

So he's a bit of a fix - er up - per, but this we're cer - tain of; you can

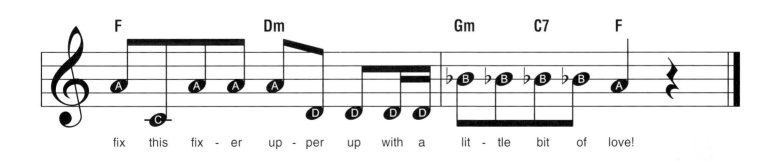

fix this fix - er up - per up with a lit - tle bit of love!

Word Search

Can you find all the music words on the list?
Circle the words you find and then cross them off the list as you work.

```
M K N D R B O O N L G E G U C S I U J I O R M
T I W W Y K A P V N D Y N A M I C S I D D T Z
G K H U M Y T J M T Q C C Z G X D V B S R Z E
T H O Z O V L P X S S A L I D G K X E H V I X
H U L C O R T I Y W M D O U B L E B A R T D T
M P E O M F D O T T E D N O T E T S M D J V C
N D N D F M I K L E D G E R L I N E K X X K U
U Y O A K Z U E O R B A O M W V O L P H K E O
R I T L K S R S T E P W L J J F T E H G I I B
E S E Y P U P I I I H O B F E G E J T F I D V
P Z N J S I B V K C B J W N M X S J R F L A T
E W Z A T F X S O M A U I M S P A C E H K C H
A Q E K I E A A Y R C L Q L W N G A B B E A U
T M U W I G M S X A D S P N M K E Q L A Y P I
S A D A D E D P E I G H T H N O T E E R B O V
I I F B R R F P O M S Q A E A P J L C L O J G
G V Q G O T C H G K C J R U I B P P L I A Y B
N U R H S R E E E H A L F N O T E N R Y L
L H C P N L F R J M L N F C A R H T F E D R I
B N X P Q U I X N U E U L I D V U B R S S B I
M C A R P E G G I O O N A L N Y S E M E T I G
H F M K X L Y K J H T I G N Q E I A F C S F E
Z H S H A R P V T I M E S I G N A T U R E T Z
```

Arpeggio	**Dynamics**	**Measure**	**Skip**
Bar lines	**Eighth note**	**Music alphabet**	**Space**
Beam	**Fine**	**Notes**	**Staff**
Beat	**Flag**	**Quarter note**	**Step**
Chord symbol	**Flat**	**Repeat sign**	**Tempo**
Coda	**Half note**	**Rest**	**Tie**
Da capo	**Keyboard**	**Rit**	**Time signature**
Dotted note	**Ledger line**	**Scale**	**Treble clef**
Double bar	**Line**	**Sharp**	**Whole note**

Answers on page 72.

Rhythm Match

Match the song titles with the rhythm that fits. One is done as an example.

__1__ Do You Want to Build a Snowman?	
____ Fixer Upper	
____ For the First Time in Forever	
____ Let It Go	
____ Lost in the Woods	
____ Some Things Never Change	
____ When I Am Older	

Answers on page 72.

Changing Meter

Sometimes the time signatures can change from one measure to the next. This is clearly marked and allows for longer and shorter phrases with different strong and weak beats. Changing meter can look tricky, but it's easy to understand. Remember which note gets the beat (often the quarter note) and notice how many beats per measure. If anything gets confusing, stop and write in the beats, as we've done in the example below.

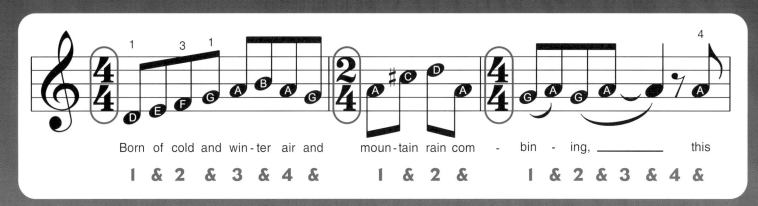

Frozen Heart

Music and Lyrics by Kristen Anderson-Lopez
and Robert Lopez

Heimr Àrnadalr
(Home Arendelle)

Music by Christophe Beck and Leo Birenberg
Lyrics by Christine Hals

For the First Time in Forever

Music and Lyrics by
Kristen Anderson-Lopez and Robert Lopez

With excitement

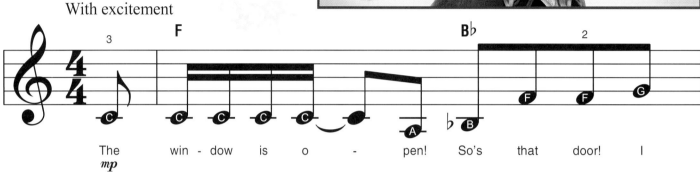

The win-dow is o-pen! So's that door! I

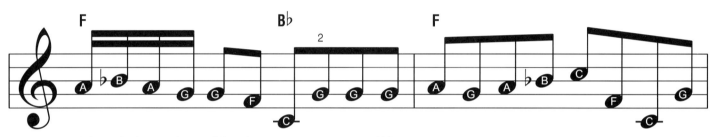

did-n't know they did that an-y-more. Who knew we owned eight thou-sand sal-ad

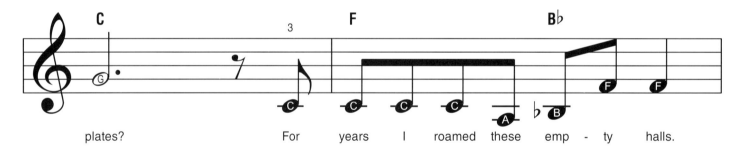

plates? For years I roamed these emp-ty halls.

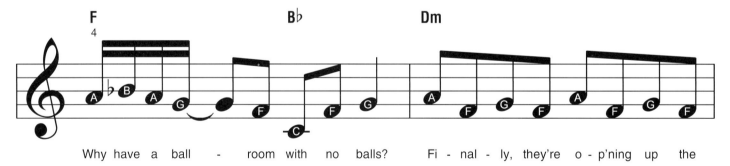

Why have a ball-room with no balls? Fi-nal-ly, they're o-p'ning up the

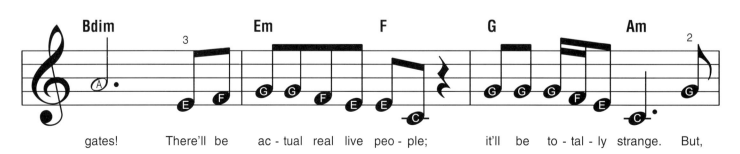

gates! There'll be ac-tual real live peo-ple; it'll be to-tal-ly strange. But,

Note Challenge

The following measures below contain pitches that spell a word.
Name the notes to discover the word.

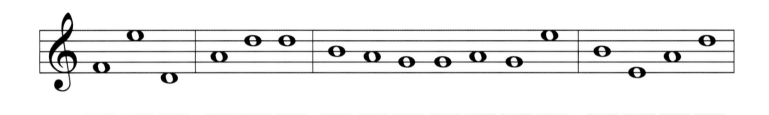

_ _ _ _ _ _ _ _ _ _ _

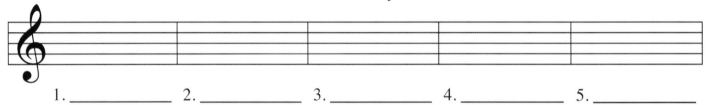

_ _ _ _ _ _ _ _ _ _ _ _

On the blank staff, create your own words.

1. _____ 2. _____ 3. _____ 4. _____ 5. _____

Answers on page 72.

Swing Eighths

"Swing" is style of music that is jazzy or bluesy in character. In this style, the eighth notes have a long-short feel, rather than a steady even feel. In the rhythm below, clap and count the eighth notes evenly.

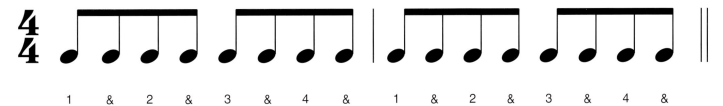

Now clap the rhythm again, this time with Swing Eighths. Listen for the shuffle feel achieved by playing the eighths as "long-short."

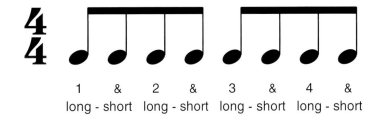

When eighth notes are to be played as swing eighths, you'll see the word "swing" or this symbol:

Practice counting these examples. Swing the eighth notes.

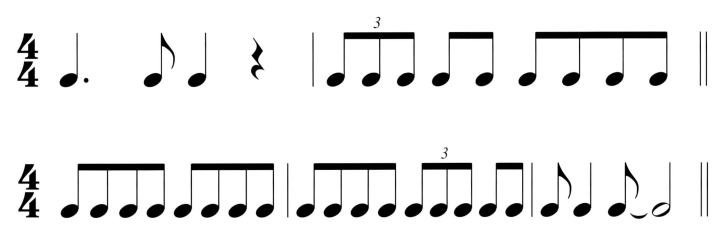

When I Am Older

Music and Lyrics by Kristen Anderson-Lopez
and Robert Lopez

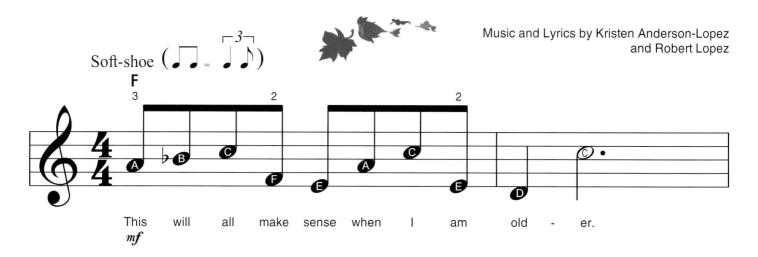

Soft-shoe

This will all make sense when I am old - er.

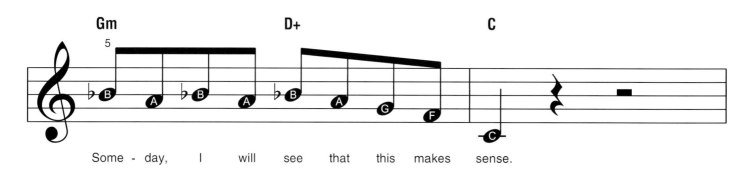

Some - day, I will see that this makes sense.

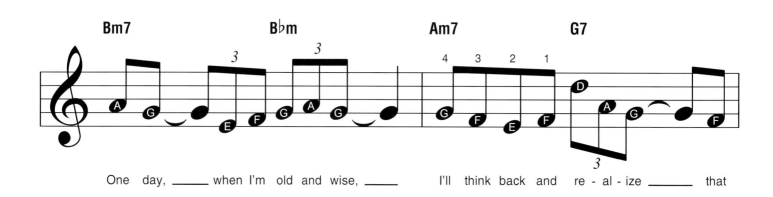

One day, _____ when I'm old and wise, _____ I'll think back and re - al - ize _____ that

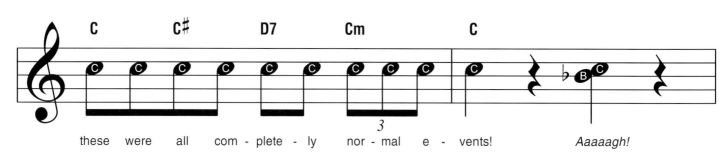

these were all com - plete - ly nor - mal e - vents! *Aaaaagh!*

F

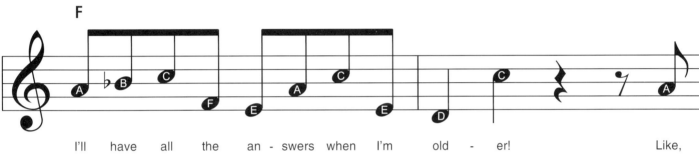

I'll have all the an - swers when I'm old - er! Like,

Gm   **D+**   **Gm**

why we're in this dark, en - chant - ed wood.

Bm7   **B♭m**   **Am7**   **Dm**

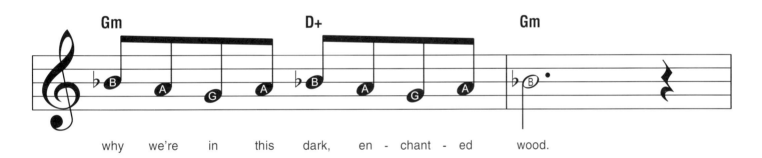

I know ____ in a cou - ple years, ____ these will seem like child - ish fears, ____ and

Gm7   **C7**   **F**

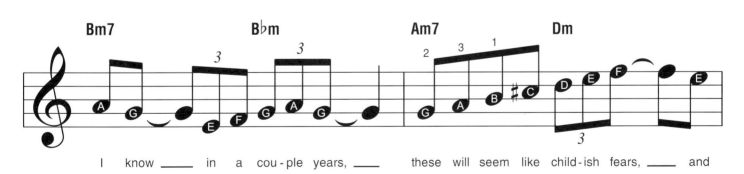

so I know, this is - n't bad, it's good!

The Next Right Thing

Music and Lyrics by Kristen Anderson-Lopez
and Robert Lopez

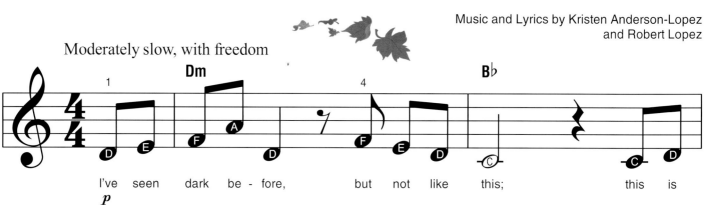

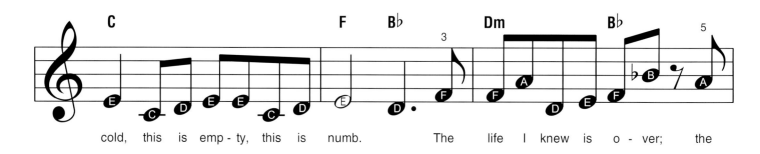

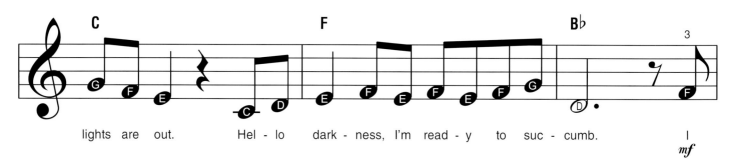

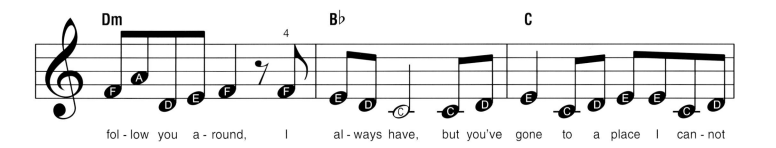

fol - low you a - round, I al - ways have, but you've gone to a place I can - not

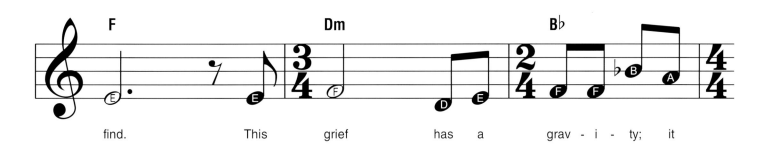

find. This grief has a grav - i - ty; it

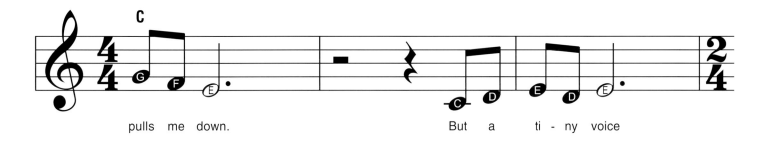

pulls me down. But a ti - ny voice

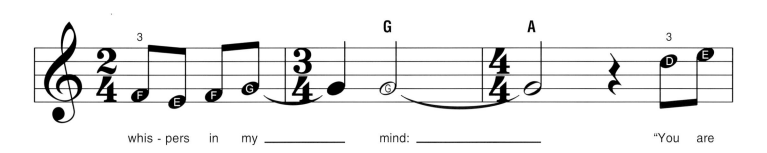

whis - pers in my _____ mind: _____ "You are

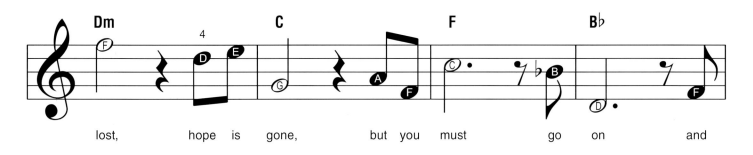

lost, hope is gone, but you must go on and

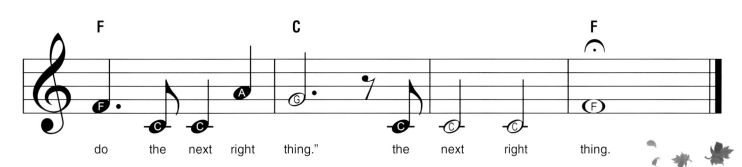

do the next right thing." the next right thing.

$\frac{6}{8}$ and $\frac{12}{8}$ Time Signatures

A time signature provides two important pieces of information. The top number indicates how many beats are in each measure. The bottom number indicates the type of note that gets one beat. Up to this point, the songs in this book have had the number 4 on the bottom.

The following rhythm example has $\frac{6}{8}$ as the time signature. Here there are six beats in a measure. The eighth note gets one beat.

The answer to Olaf's question is "both." An eighth note can be half a beat long whenever the bottom number in the time signature is 4. But in $\frac{6}{8}$ time, the eighth note gets one beat. Not only that, but in $\frac{6}{8}$ time a quarter note gets two beats. One thing never changes – two eighth notes always equal one quarter note.

Elsa's song "Into the Unknown" uses a $\frac{12}{8}$ time signature. The eighth note gets one beat, and there are 12 eighth notes in each measure. Practice clapping and counting the eighth notes.

1 - 2   3   4 - 5   6   7 - 8   9   10 - 11   12   1 - 2   3   4   5   6   7 - 8 - 9   10-11   12

You can also think of $\frac{12}{8}$ as four groups of three eighths.

1   2   3   4   1   2   3   4

Into the Unknown

Music and Lyrics by Kristen Anderson-Lopez
and Robert Lopez

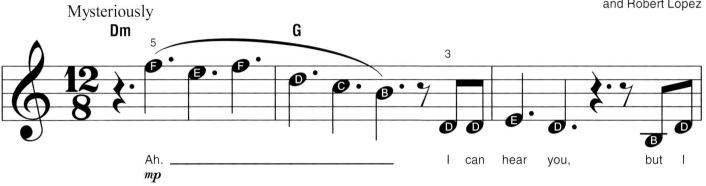

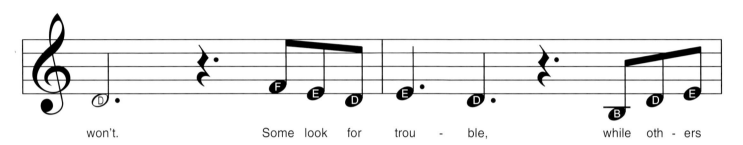

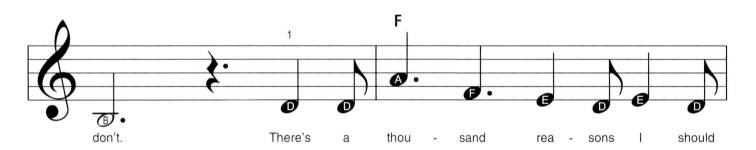

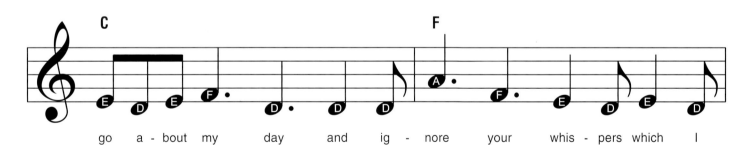

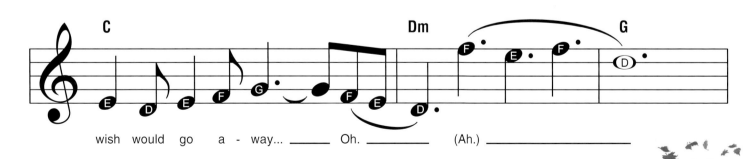

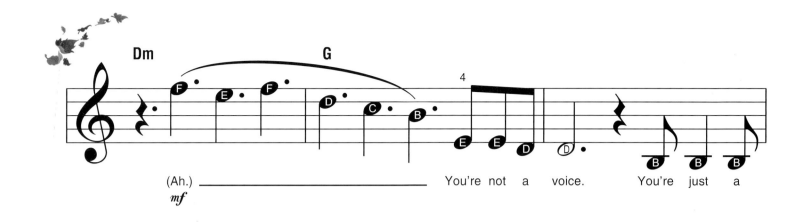

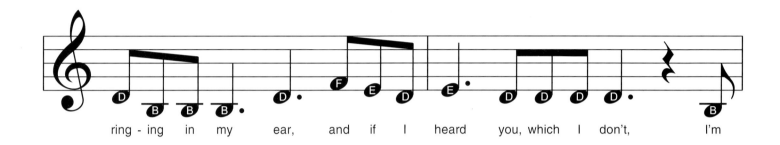

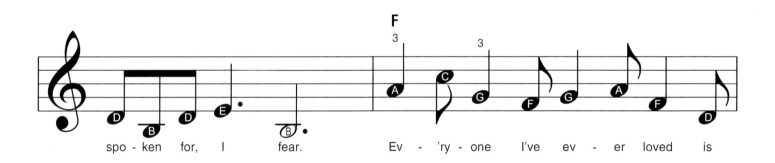

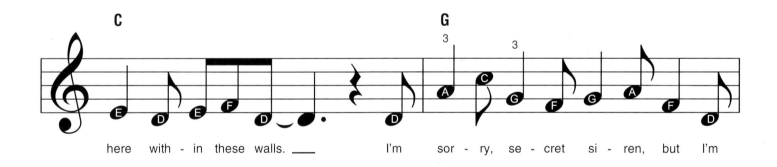

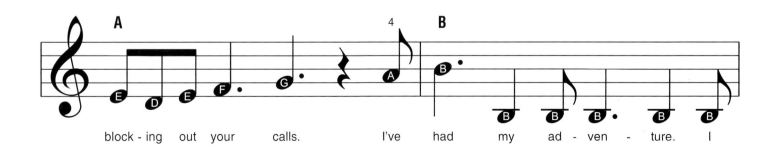

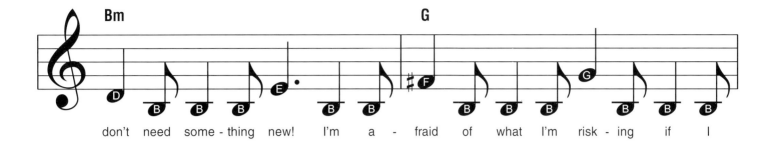

don't need some - thing new! I'm a - fraid of what I'm risk - ing if I

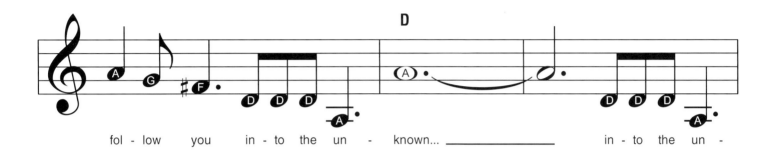

fol - low you in - to the un - known... _____ in - to the un -

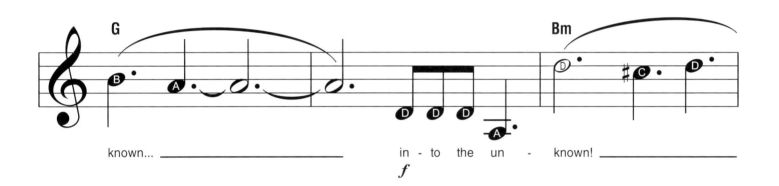

known... _____ in - to the un - known! _____

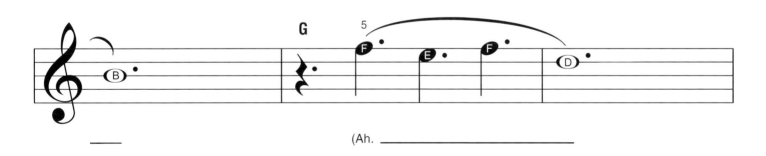

(Ah. _____

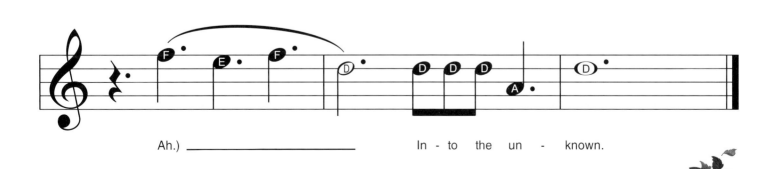

Ah.) _____ In - to the un - known.

Answer Key

p. 5 - Notes on the Staff

F A D E D A C E

F E D E G G D A D

B A G G A G E B E A D

D E E D F A C E D

B A D G E C A G E

p. 15 - Add the Missing Bar Lines

p. 16 - Rests

p. 30 - Sharp or Flat?

1.) F♯   6.) D♯
2.) D♭   7.) E♭
3.) A♭   8.) B♭
4.) C♯   9.) F♯
5.) E♭   10.) G♯

p. 31 - Crossword Fun

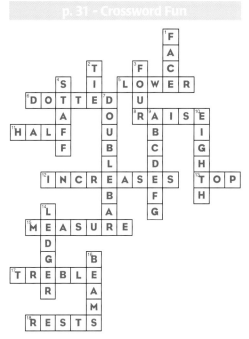

p. 32 - Music Math

2.) $1 + 1 + 1 + 1 = 4$
3.) $1 + 4 = 5$
4.) $2 + 2 + 2 + 2 = 8$
5.) $4 + 1 + 1 = 6$
6.) $2 + 2 = 4$
7.) $1 + 1 + 1 = 3$
8.) $4 + 2 = 6$
9.) $4 + 4 = 8$
10.) $4 + 1 + 2 = 7$

p. 44 - Maze Fun

p. 47 - Rest Review

1.) T   6.) T
2.) T   7.) T
3.) T   8.) T
4.) T   9.) F
5.) F   10.) F

p. 52 - Word Search

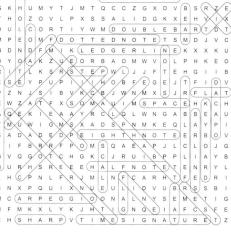

p. 53 - Rhythm Match

2.) Let It Go
3.) Some Things Never Change
4.) Fixer Upper
5.) Lost in the Woods
6.) For the First Time in Forever
7.) When I Am Older

p. 60 - Note Challenge

E G G   B E D   A G E   D E E D

F E D   A D D   B A G G A G E   B E A D